THE JOURNEY OF A POET

The Journey of a Poet
Name of the author: *Mayamol Michle*
First Published in: *2021*
©*Mayamol Michle*

MAJOR CONTENTS

PART – I
Nowhere

A Journey to the Nature and Emotions

CONTENTS

Nowhere

The bounds of my life bounded me so strong,
Not a single hole is left to escape,
The threads that so strong,
Collapsed me into a weeping heart.
Nowhere I can leave,
Nowhere I can go,
Nowhere I can take shelter,
Nowhere I can build my world.
My tears only touched the grand pastures,
My pains only hugged the soft pillow,
My palms only hold the pillar so strong,
My face only masked the fake happiness.
The time passed by days and years,
But the mask I wore is taken away,
I have learn, to live the moment,
But still exists a blankness that I left behind.

Wandering

Staring to the dark ends of long Island,
Isolated, left and abandoned,
A crooked spirit that wander,
Hisses the story of solitude.
The boundless Earth,
The boundless ocean,
The boundless sky,
Opened the doors,

To welcome the monster,
Nowhere can stay for long,
Only a visitor for a moment,
Travels backs and forth with time,
Only to confront crooked spirits.

The Blooms of Serene

The valley that widened to the ends,
The pasture that bloomed so wild,
Consumes the serene beam of energy,
The garden that blooms only in dreams,
That bloomed with the precious fragrance,
That can only be consumed,
Rarely visible or invisible,
The key of peace and calmness,
The tower of serene in vast,
Blooms the wisdom of sanctity,
That evokes precious and valuable scents,
Which can revive the dead soul,
And can renew the whole world,
That can unite all boundaries,
Which is the reason for all hidden wisdom,
A place where secret flowers blooms in serene,
And lives in all energies,
In all bouquets of heart,
In all cups of love,
That lives with the eternal being that so silent.

The Blue Whale

More deep you live,
So far your home,
But grabs hearts that watch you,
The world of ocean, so mysterious,
And you, so fortune,
Finds the danger from distance far,
Destined to knight the ocean so far,
Lives to explore the unknown oceans,
Not a single being can't escape from your knight,
All you keep is beneath the ocean,
The whales, with blue of ocean,
I wish I might be one of you,
Rather than live this terrestrial life,
Where not a single hole is left to hide.

The Last Bed

With the dark dooms, opened my eyes,
Searching for morning twilight,
The dawn is here,
But I hardly recognise, the colour of days.
Nothing is here to see,
Only the darkness wide,
That can only leave me in vain,
But, no pain, no tears,
Where not a single being can harm you,
Only remains the silence of dark doom.

Holding the last breath so long,
Fallen to the ground that so deep,
From where nobody can return,
Rests my soul deep beneath,
On a human made puff,
Decked so beautiful with flowers,
But is faded and died,
Only remains the last bed,
Where my soul rests so serene.

The Empty Pasture

The pasture so wide, vast as sky,
Stood a heaven of green world,
Peeping the beings of nature,
Recalls the days of wealth,
Once stood the trees so high,
Where blossomed the flowers of life,
Glittered the meadows of heaven,
Laid the souls of nature,
Spread the peace of dooms,
Lighted the reflects of sunshine,
Is away, far away somewhere,
From sights of being that admire,
That amazing grassland,
Where nothing else can revive,
The beauty of that wide green-land,
The admirers searched the whole world so,
Never find a place so as of that,

But the place it reigned,
Witness the pasture lifeless,
Emptied and dried.

The Murmurs of Night

The twilight has passed so long,
Only left the silent night and me,
From the distance away, heard the howling,
Flattered the bats with eyes of fire,
Farthest of the sky stood the blue star,
Blinked so bright as having a bond from births,
Reminded me that I am not alone,
The wide of skies and oceans,
Were staring at me,
The leaves of tallest of tallest trees,
Started whispering,
The voice of nature so familiar,
Even though fearful in dark,
Combines the feel of fear and calm,
Nobody can describe the harmony of night,
Nowhere else is that harmony of murmurs,
The flattering, howling and,
The unheard voices of nature.

The Divine Voice

A fountain in silence,
Incants the chants of peace,

That busses the harmony of serene nature,
Awoke the whispers undefined, from depths,
Where reigned the kingdom of vital energy,
The force behind all lives,
Sometimes, the voice of flares,
Sometimes, the voice of ocean waves,
Sometimes, the voice of silent leaves,
Sometimes, the voice of winds,
Unites the secret chants of nature divine,
Yet exists an undefined voice,
Unheard and unreachable,
The unknowns of the nature,
Those cannot be found anywhere,
Unless that unknown chant reveals,
The source of energy that possessed,
Divine and serene, of all ages,
Invisible and whole, of all boundaries,
Bright and light, of all ends,
That reverberates the voice of nature divine.

The Shadow

Broken abandoned and wounded,
But not burned to ash,
Alone wandering and sad,
But not learned to give up,
The fires of loneliness,
Burning me from foot,
A pain, that tiresome feel,

Laid me to the hands of earth,
Sleeping in the world of another,
Walking through the deserts alone,
Gliding with the blowing wind,
Looked behind in search of someone,
Nobody found, only left the shadow of mine,
Who never left me, the one that stood with me,
Always, anywhere, hidden and seen,
The curse of loneliness is so wild,
That made me rest in the shadow of mine,
Where nobody is allowed to enter,
Only the darkness that so insane.

The Last Wish

Days passes as seconds,
But the soul inside is weeping,
A lot to do but time is less,
Dreams are boundless,
Ventures are clear,
But days are counted,
Nowhere to vanish,
Only to go through,
But ways are limited,
Only the last wish exists,
That sustained in my soul,
To creep on the yards of nature,
To bloom with the wild lilies,
To fly over the wide oceans,

To explore the secret caves,
To shelter the highest mountains,
To embrace the wilderness of forest,
All I wish, is to be with nature,
Inside, silent and serene.

The Wild Darkness

A way so smooth and clear,
Bound with sorrows wild,
Creeping so tight,
Heart seems to end up beating.
A voice hidden pushes from behind,
Feeling helpless and lost,
Fallen to the hollow world,
Where exists only the darkness.
Wild and unending,
Making the vision so blind,
Not a single ray is visible,
Only the darkness wild.
Terrific than the thickness of woods,
Horrifying than the heights of mountains,
Wider than the distance of oceans,
Longer than the vastness of skies.

The Valley of Insanity

The valley that spread across the ocean of North,
Insane and serene with unique grounds,

Seat for all creatures that wild and cute,
Source of precious herbs and plants,
A valley of happiness and tears,
Stoles the heart of lovers,
Embraces the broken hearts,
And a place where poets born.
Silent and peaceful you are,
Terrific and fearful you are,
Combines the art of undefined nature,
Bonded the heights of ups and downs,
Bounded the pastures of love and pain,
So are you insane with unique bounds.

The Lonely Soul

To the distance of oceans,
Rests the untold pains,
That pierce heart on each seconds,
Nobody is near to console,
Only the speechless eyes,
Not a single being to hold,
Only the wide pastures seen,
Broken and torn is the heart,
But not ready to give up,
A voice from the depths,
Tries to encourage the soul,
Lonely, locked and shattered,
Bounded only with the feelings,
Of being alone and abandoned,

Wishes to fall on hell,
But a voice of soul,
Deep inside whispers,
To leave for somewhere,
'Where you are just a visitor.'

To My Soulmate

To the vast of skies, I searched for you,
Only seen you with the voice of heart,
Owned you within the secret chambers of heart,
But never got a chance to find you,
So strange is the feeling that I had for you,
Born the feelings without my consent,
But is true and real,
That I have feelings for you,
From the bottom of my heart,
Feels that you also experiences as mine,
You might be in a distance,
That I can never reach,
But you are nailed to my heart,
From where emits the pure love,
Even though I never found you anywhere,
Hopes, you are there somewhere,
A day of ours can unite us,
Arises a voice, unique from heart.

Rain

To the flowers bloomed in,
To the birds chirping in,
To the breeze that passes by,
I say, you are mine.
In you, I find peace and warmth,
Even though you are cool,
Each tiny drop of you makes me float,
The smooth touch of you makes me fly.
Even the last day of mine,
Wishes to stay with you,
The pastures were I lie,
Should be clouded by you.

The Murmurs

The leaves at the north end,
Always enchants a hymn,
The one I ever tried to understand,
Which always remains a mystery,
Beyond the hills and oceans,
I searched for the meaning,
But never found anything,
Clueless, confused and tired,
I walked towards the ocean,
Heard the murmurs again,
Found the fountain of enchants,
But not the leaves,
It's the nature that always spoke to me.

Rain Drops

Sleeping for the ages that define,
The chronicles of mankind,
Barely heard the voice of cracking,
But not understand what it is,
Something cool touched my cheeks,
Dreaming interpreted it as snow,
As I opened my eyes found its raining,
The rain drops were filtered by a wind,
touching my cheeks, letting me awake,
Letting my hands to hold the rain drops,
My heart travelled to ages back,
Even the most thing I considered,
These rain drops can be disappeared by time,
And can reappear with the time,
Even though this rain makes me feel,
I have a soul within me.

Wings

To the wings of my mind, hear me,
I wish I might fly,
To the ends of the northern sky,
And embrace the blanket of clouds,
Be a companion to the birds high,
Glide the beams in a second,
Find the mysterious paths,
View the land from the above,

See the wilderness of oceans,
Absorb the nativity of woods,
And feel the serenity of winds.

The Lost Dream

Some dreams are behind the curtains,
The one that most precious,
The one that can let me smile,
The one that always drive me,
My dreams were my strength,
I remember, the day I lost my dream,
Piercing my heart into pieces,
And letting me down to hell,
For the first time, I weeped from my heart,
For the first time, I blamed myself,
And it was the first time, I yelled on mine,
It was of you, my lost dream.

The Star

From the heaven, the most-high,
You are shining with dark doom,
Staring the Earth sky,
Mirrors the ocean with bright dots,
To the vast of the galaxy,
You pretends to be nothing,
Though the sky is decked by you,
As the diamond, most brightest,

The ages you passed,
The ocean you mirrored,
The sky you reigned,
Says, you are the brightest.

The Blue Bird

Your wings takes you to the mount most highest,
You have your nests on the cliffs where no one can reach,
There is no numbers and limits, the oceans you explored,
There is no woods and jungle, that you lived for once,
You have your companions everywhere,
You have the wisdom of peace in you,
There is no other creature in this world like you,
The oceans you crossed,
The woods you passed,
The cliffs you lived,
The mounts you flied,
Says, you are blue and you are free.

The Mount of North East

The mount of the north east that stood in courage,
The head doomed with the skies above,
The palms opens into the fountains,
The foot reigns over the creatures unknown,

To the highest of the vast sky, spreaded the surface,
Letting no one to measure, no one to know,
The secret chambers and treasures that holds,
The precious stone glitters with the moon sky,
Is shattered all over the surface,
Letting itself to be another moon,
With the floating lighters from the pastures far.

The Faded

In all creatures, in all worlds,
You are the most prettiest,
From the first day of your birth,
Your glow and charm covered everyone,
No one of the planet is unaware of you,
No one can avoid you, unless they are blind,
You were given for the welcomes,
You were handed for new beginnings,
You were shared for lifelong bounds,
You were holded for the last journey,
To the end of you, let others,
found joy with you,
You were wounded, scratched and thrown,
You reigned the world of dreams,
Even though you are wounded,
You were taken from mother branch, as a bud,
And blossomed into the hands of humans,
They picked you from home,
and left you to new worlds with wounds,

Your beauty, left them in trance,
And you are sent to the coffins for the rests,
And even thrown, as you lost your glow,
My faded rose.

The Crust

Chambers deep inside,
spelled with the magical trance of past,
place unknown to the beings of terrestrial,
the core of all secrets,
the heir of mourning explodes,
the yard of mysterious darkness,
the home of secret furnaces,
the world of unexplored heeps,
the stone of energy blocks,
surrounded with the rocky knights,
protected with the weiry cloud underneath,
and shielded with icy hands,
the ways of four chambers with the golden doors,
opens to the unknown worlds,
from where nobody has returned,
the chambers opens to the four wild kingdoms,
the kingdom of oceans,
the kingdom of rocks,
the kingdom of fire,
and the kingdom of unknown,
reasoned for all life energies.

The Sunrise

The first rays of twilight touched my cheeks,
from the window at the end,
the rays reached me traveling a long journey,
the coldness of morning was leaving,
but the music of birds has begun,
the leaves were shedding dewdrops.
Moving to the window opened,
feeling the twilight,
I felt the yard to be heaven,
the sun in the eastern sky,
rising from the depths of sea,
it seems that the world has no end.
The doors of the window seem to be magical,
each time it opens, feels the presence of an energy
that is serene,
to the vast of the window was empty,
far away, only bushes and birds,
the visibility of sunrise is not hard to catch,
within the bushes there is a way that ends on the
fountain,
this makes me feel that I am in sky each time,
a heaven of my own.

To the Star in the Night Sky

From the distant fars of sky,
You blinked so bright,

Wiping the doom of darkest nights,
Captures the heart of lonely beings.
The beam of your narrow rays,
Brings hope in the narrow path,
Your blinks shines as fire,
Who always wanted to fall on Earth.
You exposes the serenity of vast skies,
And enlight the charms of night sky,
I always wanted you beside me,
Cause, you are the one who is nearest to me,
In all darkness and silence.

The Red Moon

The valley you lighted, the seas you mirrored,
The eyes you decked, said you are insane,
The sight you glimpsed before me,
Took my heart with you,
Even you are red, you are not,
You are the one, most precious,
Reflects the rocky surface,
With a glow of thousand stars,
The eyes that watched you,
Always said, you are beautiful,
But today, you are insane,
For me, the ages and nature,
You are the serene in doom,
And lives in the heart of chants,
Of the unknown world, unknown history.

The Being, Eternal

My heart always wanted for a search,
The search for the extreme peace,
The one that existed in the hollow world,
The one that still exists deep inside me.
I am in search of the being that is eternal,
Something that reigns above the senses,
The knowledge that fills on each atom,
The energy that bounds the whole universe.
Striving to reach the reality,
I crave for the being that above,
In all creations, the pure and serene,
In all being, that alive and dead.
To the most peak, I have searched,
Never find anyone who is eternal,
To the rest, I gave up,
I found, that being is the nature.
The nature is the soul of all energies,
The being eternal, the energy,
That relies in all beings,
In all atoms, in all senses.

A Letter

To the brightest star in the sky,
the boundless sky above,
doomed with tiny dots of blinks,

who captures the heart of the lonely,
the one that is destined,
to explore the crooked world,
who reigns the night sky so proudly,
serving as the deck of the dark blanket,
I, the fatal human wishes that,
I might be one of your admirers,
who spread across the universe.

The Faded Star

The nights that I wandered,
for a tiny ray of hope,
risen the star so bright,
distant and far,
blooming the fragrance,
of a vibrant spirit in me,
making my soul calm and quiet.
Waited for a single sight so long,
not visible a tiny twinkle,
only vast cloudy sky and me,
from the farthest seen a faded light,
that buried with the darkest dooms,
a star that always lit up light in me,
is doomed to the hands of a cloudy curse.

The Flower of Eden

The garden most beautiful,

The rosary of all flowers,
The bouquet of all fruits,
The heaven of Earth,
In you blossoms the world's prettiest flowers,
In you, it is living,
In you, it is nurtured,
In you, it is glowing,
In you, it is colored,
Within you, it is protected,
Within you, it is kept,
Within you, it is faded,
Within you, it is died,
To the beauty of you, it is reborn,
To the praise of you, it is renovated,
To the sanctity of you, it is remained,
To the prosperity of you, it is replenished,
O, the flower of Eden,
Cute and serene,
You are the beauty of Eden.

The Shadow

The shades of your vast branches,
The tender leaves with chants,
The silent prayers of your soul,
Lead me to the ground where you stood.
To the vast of the surface,
I searched for you,
I missed the days of my hanging,

And the days of my naps on your branch.
Leaving to the days back,
I can only remember the music of birds,
That always played on my ears as lullaby,
But today, exists only the shadows of memories.
The pasture you stood is empty,
The birds on you is vanished,
The tenderness of you is wiped,
The highness of you is nowhere.

Tears of My Heart

Each drop of my tears,
Recites the pain of my heart,
That is broken and lost,
In the valleys of pains.
A ray of hope,
That was visible from the far,
Is found to be an illusion,
A sight that so fake.
Wanted my heart to smile,
But it was drowned so deep,
To the depths of unending misfortunes,
Leaving only a tearful eye.

The Drowning Spirit

To the blue skies afar,
To the oceans wide,

To the woods deepest,
To the pastures green,
Want to say the story of a soul,
Who wanted to live in you,
Who wished to rest on you,
Some lives seems so strange,
That never ends the hardships,
That follows as a curse.
Being hopeless,
Mourning and weeping,
Left the days many,
But the zone of comfort never reached,
Only the darkness infinite,
Doomed so wild,
Not a single ray of hope visible,
Tired, torn and wandering,
Turned the soul,
Never reached a shelter of hope.
Being abandoned to the fate,
Merciless and cruel,
Made the spirit on darkness of depths,
From where nobody can come back,
Fallen deep inside surrounding,
The assassins of fate,
Bounded to the fence of drooping,
Where, one cannot take a breath,
Left only the long way of darkness,
That embraces to an unending journey.

Unhealed

From the depths of oceans,
From the wilderness of woods,
From the vastness of skies,
From the wide of deserts,
I searched for healings,
Never found a one,
The weeps of my heart,
Never healed and risen,
From the wounds of past,
I only tried to heep it on mine,
The time passed witnessed,
Some wounds never heal.

The Time Has changed

The wind that blown,
gently reminds me the days passed,
the charming and senseless days,
the cute mistakes and fights,
the time has travelled in a moment,
leaving those days unfulfilled,
but my heart insists to stay back,
is insisting on something impossible,
the time has passed and nothing is as before,
everything is changed without leaving a sign.

A Day for You

The wounds that heals in silence,
Restores the energy that lost in doom,
Hopeless, mourning and weeping days,
Passes with time.
From the distance of light years,
From the heights of unexplored mountains,
From the depths of oceans,
Comes the rays of hope,
The days of tears and miseries,
The days of pain and wounds,
The days of silence and despair,
Decks a day for you.

The Serene

The window that opens to the fountain,
The door that explores all wisdom,
The spell that embrace all energies,
The tunnel that ends up in deep worlds.
Serene, silent and peace,
Visible and invisible,
Well furnished from the very beginning,
The hidden world of fate.
Nobody can invade you,
Nobody can reach you,
But only the infinite soul,
Who is pure and serene.

The Scattered Dream

The first rays of morning,
Reached me so early,
Woke in a light so bright,
That left me blind,
The winks were searching,
For the pieces of dream,
That scattered on the sparks of rays.
A dream that seems so familiar,
Companion from days and years,
Lost in a single flash of sun,
The secret dream,
That I always hide in me,
Peeps out as a thief,
To get in back to the memories passed.
But, as the dream broke with sunshine,
The dream that I hided to mine,
Also gone, scattered and vanished,
With the time and days.

Your Days

Leave your sorrows to time,
Leave your pains to heal,
Leave your tears to wipe out,
And leave your miseries to fate.
The days that so calm,

The days that so charm,
The days that so hopeful,
Is on the way.
The days yet to come may be yours,
Never let your spirit down,
The days of your agonies,
Makes days that brings happiness.

Faking

Staring to the life that so disgusting,
The murmurs that so piercing,
Always echoes on my ears,
The fake smiles,
The fake concerns,
The fake emotions,
Are all I received.
The echoes of passed days,
Murmured with a pierce,
Nothing is real,
Faking is everywhere.

Dreams to

I wish I can build a place,
Where I can dwell with all my heart,
A place of my own,
Very personal and protected,
From the crooked eyes,

That looks for my fall,
Though I am nothing,
I lived the life in dream,
Where I have a heaven of my own,
Where I am the only human,
Happy and peaceful,
With the gifts of nature,
Only one wish remains,
That this dream may never end.

Pain and Gain

The days that passes,
Is not less than a disaster,
A pain that pierce my heart,
Even still exists a fire of hope,
That enchants the ends of pain,
A lantern that can guide,
To the dreams that are dead,
Which can revive the dead,
So as for the days of gains,
That awaits to pay back.

Night Sky

Decked so bright with diamonds precious,
Chants the melody of serene world,
Captures the heart of the blooming flower,
Enlightens the soul of crooked spirit,

Harmonize the rhythm of night world,
Directs the dawn and dusk,
Hilarious and marvelous at the same time,
So is the night sky.

The Depth of a Well

Looking deep inside,
trembled my heart with fear,
sufferings those I come across,
are tends to be meaningless,
the more I strengthened myself,
rose the vains of pain,
wanted to end the endless pain,
but have no courage to make it,
stood long before the old well,
surrounded with fallen leaves,
to drown myself, to elope from pains,
but a voice inside never allowed me,
instead buried me in fear,
the eyes that filled with tears,
dropped one or more,
memorizing the hardships I gone through,
I can't end this life like this,
I should live for my dreams,
for the tears that I shed for them.

Tears of Heaven

The eyes glittered with tears,
tired are they, but glowing intensely,
tears never ended up,
it shared the companionship of loneliness,
staring sky afar, the cloudy bed,
dripped a drop so tiny,
to hide the tears of mine,
like the heaven descended to wipe out,
like the skies shares my pain,
as of someone send from heaven,
to comfort this lonely soul.

The Hollow Mind

When I think of the days passed,
flares the rays of tears,
unknown was the pain,
when I was living it,
wanted to reach a shore,
where I can find me,
to revive the dead days passed,
leaning to the depths of ocean,
there is only the never reached depth,
making my mind a blank slate,
where I can only see the hollow core.

Featherless Bird

The time has passed so long,

still I am looking for my dreams,
they are out of reach and far,
but my heart still craves for it,
like a featherless bird I am,
lost my dreams and soul,
in the depths of never ending path,
dark, scary and unrevealed,
a curse of heaven to know,
the bitterness of pain and humiliation.

The Cloudy Sky

Far above the mounts,
reigned you so proud,
making the earthly beings jealous,
even the vultures can't reach you,
far and high were you,
the height of mountains,
were not enough to compete with you,
but you have proven,
that the heaven of highs,
got it's creation from you,
with your never ending vastness,
you have stolen the beings of earth,
to dream a day with you,
gliding and floating,
on your soft layers,
cool and stunning.

Misty Morning

The silence of night were broken,
far afar rises a new morning,
with all its charms and beauty,
the mounts around seems to be heaven,
with the long spread mists,
like a bed of clouds,
cool and miraculous were they,
the top of tallest trees,
were buried with its vastness,
they were spread across the woods,
oceans, mounts and valleys,
fallen slowly the rays of sun,
absorbed and vanished the white,
only remained a hope,
to meet these cloud beds,
on another day, another morning.

The Serene of Tears

When the happiest days of life,
Fades and disappears,
Unaware was the soul,
The creeps of misfortunes,
Grabbed so tight,
The threads of life,
Were broken and abandoned,
Left only the corners broken,

As a curtain to shed all the tears,
Not a single drop is left,
Only left the blankness,
Of long serenity born from the tears.

Deserts of Mind

Like the vastness of deserts,
My heart is being wandering,
Into the never ending ways of life,
Never thought about failures,
But the fate is unpredictable,
Showered all the misfortunes,
Like a heavy rain,
Making my soul to wander,
Around dried pastures,
Who were once green,
And now a sand-filled desert.

Star of the Night Sky

The blanket of dark dooms,
Cannot take your glimpse from me,
To the highest of all clouds,
Reigns you with numerous companions,
Some rock, some dust, some light,
And at the most farthest, you.

My eyes always founded you,

Even in the clouded bed sky,
Your glimpses can't escape from my sight,
For the world, you are just a star,
For me you are my best friend, my companion,
In the most darkest skies, I can see you,
I can feel your slight blinks and cold,
Though I miss you in all rains.

Phoenix

The history of faded memories,
The petals that fallen from,
The ancient era,
The nights wounded at the doors,
Of farthest skies,
The burned page of enlightened wisdom,
Recalls the courage of the knight,
Who flied up from the ash,
The oceans of the vast chambers,
The drowned kingdoms,
Praises the glory of that knight,
Who stood up in fire,
The knight who embraced,
The strong darkness of red rubies,
Hot, piercing and melting,
The cells into lava,
None of the feathers, the eyes,
Can be pierced melted or doomed,
Stood up the knight, from the,

Terrible hands of dark dooms,
Flattering the ashes and,
Flew into the sky in a moment,
Letting witness the resurrection of,
A phoenix.

Euphoric Love

The blue sky afar knows,
The mesmerizing touch of love,
The craves of attention,
And the longing for togetherness,
Making the self, vanish in love,
No sense of present and future,
Only the time being together,
Making each-others smile,
And sometimes fighting,
As sedated to love,
Making you as,
The cause of my euphoria.

The End

PART -II

The Feathers of

Winter

*A Journey to the Colours of
Winter…*

CONTENTS

The Feathers of Winter

In the misty sky of winter,
With the soft tiny dewdrops,
I felt I am floating on the sky,
With the faded memories of past.
The breeze that humbly hugged me,
Remind me that, once I was free,
The leaf that fallen from above,
Took me to the world of fascinations.
The bird that loses the winter feathers,
Can revive those with time,
With more beauty and colour,
With more softness and tender.
The feather that flew towards the ground,
May never had a pain,
But is meant for the restoration,
Of an existing fantasy.
I wish I might be a bird,
Who can revive from shedding feathers,
And fly with the wings that restored,
To the ends of the boundless world.

The Melody of Winter

From the cloudy sky of winter,
Rarely made the stars visits,
The moon somewhere shined as blue,
But the melody of winter night never faded.

From the skies afar sheds the precious hails,
Made the tropic a snowball,
The morning let the dews vanish,
But the night, brought them back.

From the corners of my heart,
Raises the craving for the winter night,
That so pretty, quiet and peaceful,
With the melody of white snows.

Staring to the winter sky,
The dips of snow, whiter and tiny,
Possess a harmony of serenity that unexplainable,
That letting my heart, leap with joy.

The winter days itself possess, a silent hymn,
That nobody can hear,
Only the one with the blessings of mysterious
power,
Can hear that voice of serene winter.

The Winter Flower

In the silence of winter, blossoms the purest soul,
So pretty and soft are your petals,
Even the heaven can't imagine your beauty,
You made the valleys so beautiful,
Your decks may have no bound,

That you are even found in narrowest places,
Your existence have recognition,
 Even in the woods, that so dark and deep.
Not a single being can ignore you,
Cause you are blossomed from the heart of nature,
You are the heavenly bliss, that lights beauty,
You can creep on yards and tunnels,
You are blessed to grow so wild,
So as you ornament the nature so pure,
You can shine as jewels that blossomed in peace,
The farthest skies and darkest dooms,
Praises your beauty and purity,
So are you the winter flower,
Blossoms under the misty cloud,
With the blessings of skies afar.

The Shades of Winter

The night decked like a groom,
charm and young,
Only the white pastures seen,
to the distance,
Glows with the precious moonlight,
making the Earth another moon.
The moonlight fell on the trees side,
mend a shadow on the other,
The shades seems to be a shelter,
where I can burry my weeping heart,
in the silence of the serene winter.

Let the leaf fallen to the shades,
be my companion to next day,
The moon from the east,
stood so long to bring myself,
to the shades of winter,
Thought that the time won't pass,
unless my tears got wiped out.

The Winter Dream

To be in moon, to be in venus,
Is a dream that fascinates soul,
The winter reminds the fascinated soul,
That the moon itself falls to earth,
In the silence of winter days,
Visits the venus, with the chants of love,
Reviving the beauty of sleeping earth,
Only the frozen ocean can remember,
The hardness of winter,
Only the tiny leaf can know,
The winter's finger of death,
Where, I am sleeping with blankets of dreams,
That are possessed to the winter days,
The white pastures that so light and soft,
The silent night sky that so pretty and glaring,
Delighted the dark soul of mine, that fantasized,
On the edge of dream so serene and fearful,
Lifted to the thoughts of sacrifice,
Of that fallen leaf and frozen ocean.

The Winter Bird

Frozen the winter so hard,
Flied to the oceans wide for warmth,
Made shelters on grounds beneath,
Brood for warmth and safeness,
Never complained the freeze of winter,
Embraced the finger of nature,
Fell down the feather that was old,
But revived in new colours,
My wings so small, but are fires,
Can travel to the ocean too distant,
Can explore the hidden mountains and caves,
Can take shelters in fearful woods,
Never afraid about the frozen winter,
Never lived on the thoughts of ends,
Never sung the song of death, so that,
I am the winter bird.

The Winter Night

With the white pastures that spread along,
The life of Earth so miraculous,
With the sky beds in heights,
The beauty of Earth is so delightful,
Possessed with the night sky so,
Eyes wandering for the little souls,
Who blinks with tiny twinkles,
Relies my world of thoughts,

The moon brightest in the sky,
Captured the heart so pure,
Poured the droplets of love,
Which blown a seductive power,
Melody of nightingale,
Visitors of the night sky,
Strange and fearful noise of beings,
Lit up the trance of winter night,
That so mysterious.

The Frozen Winter

The Northern sky seem,
to be wordless,
Frozen is the land,
and silent is the beings,
Remains only the murmurs,
of falling snow,
Freezing the nature with love.
Caves and ground,
the branches of highest trees,
Embraced the winter,
with its frozen hands,
The symphony of winter,
revived so bright,
Leaving the North,
frozen and rocky.
Though is the winter,
though is my heart,

Frozen with cold memories,
and reminders,
Let this freeze of winter,
be the cure of my pain,
Where I can burry mine,
in the valleys frozen.

The Winter Soulmate

Found you from the depths of icy mountain,
The silent hisses of your words,
Buried the thoughts of ages in mine,
Not a single channel to express,
What my heart is clinging to,
The coldness of winter, brought you here,
And vanished with the winter.

Long ago I heard your voice,
But I expects you in all moments,
Cause I found my soulmate in you,
The angel, one that fallen from heavens,
Came from the cloudy mists,
So you are known as the snow angel,
Who disappears with the winter cycle,
I wish you might be with me in all life,
Holding me, guiding me, to the paths unknown.

The Winter Rain

Stood the land alike to a heaven,
Peaceful, serene and pure,
Snowy land so whitest,
Brought the angels so admirable.
Fallen to the ground an angel,
Cursed to be a human,
Lived the life on tears,
That bound on unending miseries.
Even the days are buried on winter,
Rains the heart so badly,
Making the days annoying,
Harder and Scattered.
A rain of tears never ended,
Being condemned and compassioned,
Sorrowful and tearful,
Passed the days, left in unending rain.

The Winter Day

Staring at the winter clouds,
leaps my heart so strange,
to embrace the daring rays of,
prince, young and charm.
The blankets of colourless worlds,
faded and lean,
covered him from my sight,
leaving my soul alone,
in the banks of river,
that flows on his direction.
The breeze that so soft,

touched me for a moment,
letting me in trance of,
the unknown feeling.
The charming days of winter,
flashed mysteriously on my memory,
letting me drive to the past,
where I am floated with nature,
embracing the serene world,
that spells the chants of love.

The Winter Dawn

From the morning warmth,
Stood the sun so charming,
In the east of the coast afar,
Buried in winter shines,
Seems that the sun is sleeping,
As a child bounded with blankets.
The clouds spread all over the sky,
Seems that heaven descends,
But the heart is not quiet,
Wanted to fly over the clouds,
To meet the hidden prince,
But its not a fairytale.
To recite the story of descended,
But desires to be a fairy.

The Winter Fire

In this snow falling night,
the coldness of winter has spread everywhere,
but not on the suffering human heart,
that longing for a door to open,
to rebuild the broken walls of heart,
where a senseless pain arises always,
that pierce the wounds yet to heal,
but there is no room for complains,
the breathless soul inside weeps,
the pain it caused becomes a cure,
letting a fire burn inside,
to heal the wounds of heart,
with the ways that directs to hope.

The End

Be Hopeful and Happy with nature…